CONTENTS

KT-529-092

FALKIRK COUNCIL
LIBRARY SUPPORT
FOR SCHOOLS

LORD ALAN SUGAR

'You're fired!'. Lord Alan Sugar gradually reduces 16 eager contestants to one winner on the reality TV programme *The Apprentice*. The show represents the harsh and ruthless business world that this shrewd entrepreneur has thrived in.

Alan Sugar receives the Best Feature award for his series *The Apprentice* at the British Academy Television Awards.

YOUNG ENTREPRENEUR

Sugar left school at 16. He briefly had a job in the **civil service**, but soon realised his skills lay in business. He began selling car aerials and electric goods from the back of his old van. In 1968, at the age of 21, he set up an electrical goods company called Amstrad (which stands for Alan Michael Sugar Trading).

HOME AND BUSINESS

In the mid-'80s Sugar was selling inexpensive home computers – by the million. At its peak in 1987, Amstrad was worth £1.2 billion. By the early 1990s Amstrad's latest range of computers had technical problems and sales suffered. However, Sugar was not deterred. The company began producing different products, including video recorders, DVD players and satellite TV **receiver boxes**.

GROWING COMPANY

The satellite receiver box business was very **lucrative** for Amstrad during the 1990s and 2000s. 75 per cent of the sales were to the satellite TV company BSkyB (previously Sky). Wanting to focus on other business interests, such as property **investment**, Sugar sold Amstrad to BSkyB in 2007 for around £125 million.

CELEB STATUS

Sugar maintains his high-profile status with the popular TV show *The Apprentice*. Every year he employs the TV show's winner in a suitable role within one of his companies. He relishes the opportunity to inspire young people to become entrepreneurs. The **spin-off** series *Junior Apprentice* features competitors between the ages of 16 and 17.

'I can tell you where every screw, nut and bolt is in my company. I know everything [in my business]. Never, ever, underestimate me.'

372968

CELEB★

ENTREPRENEURS

GEOFF BARKER

FRANKLIN WATTS

LONDON·SYDNEY

First published in 2011 by
Franklin Watts
338 Euston Road
London NW1 3BH

Franklin Watts Australia
Level 17/207 Kent Street
Sydney NSW 2000

© 2011 Franklin Watts

ISBN: 978 1 4451 0534 5

Dewey classification number: 338'04'0922

All rights reserved.

A CIP catalogue record for this book is available from the British Library.

Planning and production by Discovery Books Limited
Managing Editor: Laura Durman
Editor: James Nixon
Designer: D.R. ink

Printed in China

Franklin Watts is a division of Hachette Children's Books, an Hachette UK company.
www.hachette.co.uk

Photo acknowledgements: Getty Images: pp. 6 (Gareth Davies), 10 (FilmMagic/Jon Kopaloff), 18 (ABC/Holly Farrell), 22–23 (Justin Sullivan), 25 (WireImage/Brian Ach), 27 (Sondeep Shankar); Photoshot: pp. 3 and 18–19 (Face to Face/Starstock), 11 (Starstock/Gary Lee), 13 (UPPA/Sanjay Jha), 16 (Picture Alliance/Jens Buettner), 20 (Rune Hellestad), 21 (Brian Jordan), 23 (Sony Pictures), 26–27 (Olivier Douliery); Rex Features: pp. 7 (Ken McKay), 9 (Startraks Photo), 14–15 (Justin Williams), 15 (Jonathan Hurdle); Shutterstock Images: pp. 5, 8 (Helga Estreb), 12 (Chris Mansfield), 17 (Jaggat); Wikimedia: pp. 24 (LGEPR).

Cover photos: Getty Images: Oprah Winfrey (WireImage/Don Arnold); Rex Features: Lord Alan Sugar (Brian J Ritchie); Shutterstock Images: Bill Gates.

Every attempt has been made to clear copyright. Should there be any inadvertent omission, please apply to the Publishers for rectification.

To the best of its knowledge, the Publisher believes the facts in this book to be true at the time of going to press. However, due to the nature of celebrity, it is impossible to guarantee that all the facts will still be current at the time of reading.

Note to parents and teachers: Every effort has been made by the Publishers to ensure that the websites in this book are suitable for children, that they are of the highest educational value, and that they contain no inappropriate or offensive material. However, because of the nature of the Internet, it is impossible to guarantee that the contents of these sites will not be altered. We strongly advise that Internet access is supervised by a responsible adult.

The famous finger of Alan Sugar that tells contestants on his TV show *The Apprentice* if they have won or lost the competition.

FACT

Lord Sugar was chairman of football club Tottenham Hotspur during the 1990s, which he later described as 'a waste of my life'.

CELEB BIO

Date of birth **24 March 1947**

Place of birth **London, UK**

Launched first company **1968**

Approximate wealth **£730 million**

OPRAH WINFREY

'You know you are on the road to success if you would do your job and not get paid for it.'

Oprah Winfrey's chat show has had ongoing success for 25 years.

FACT

When Oprah was 17 years old, she was the winner of the Miss Black Tennessee beauty pageant.

Oprah Winfrey has interviewed many big names, including pop star Christina Aguilera.

CELEB BIO

Date of birth **29 January 1954**

Place of birth **Kosciusko, Mississippi, USA**

Launched first company **1986**

Approximate wealth **£2.7 billion**

Known and admired for her honest, direct approach on her TV chat show, Oprah Winfrey is considered by many to be one of the most influential women in the USA today. Respected as a powerful media mogul, Oprah is also the richest self-made woman in the United States.

DIFFICULT CHILDHOOD

Oprah experienced a very difficult childhood. At the age of 14 she became pregnant, but her baby died shortly after birth. She hit the headlines in 1985, when *The Oprah Winfrey Show* tackled the sensitive subject of sexual abuse. A tearful Oprah admitted in front of TV cameras that she had been raped as a nine-year-old by a family member.

YOUNG MILLIONAIRE

Oprah first worked as a TV news reporter. In 1984 she set up a morning chat show in Chicago. The following year it was named *The Oprah Winfrey Show*. By 1986 Oprah's successful show had gone national, making her a millionaire. She quickly became the highest-paid chat show host ever, earning over $30 million in 1987. Working with boundless energy, her dream was to become 'the richest black woman in the world'.

IN COMPLETE CONTROL

In 1986 Oprah founded the media production company Harpo (Oprah spelt backwards). She proved herself to be a strong, natural businesswoman. In 1988 her company took over ownership of *The Oprah Winfrey Show*, producing it at Harpo Studios.

She has since expanded her media empire to include top women's lifestyle publication *O, The Oprah Magazine* and her website Oprah.com.

BATTLES WITH WEIGHT

As a celebrity, Oprah is constantly in the public eye. She has struggled with weight problems. In one show, she famously showed off her new figure – having lost 30 kilograms. Over the years Oprah's weight has yo-yoed up and down. Oprah chooses to use her experiences positively. She co-wrote a best-selling book about weight loss called *Make the Connection: Ten Steps to a Better Body and a Better Life*.

SIMON COWELL

Due to the success of his TV productions in the UK and the USA, Cowell is a star on both sides of the Atlantic.

'Work hard, be patient and be a sponge while you're learning your business. Learn how to take criticism. Follow your gut instincts and don't compromise.'

CELEB BIO

Date of birth **7 October 1959**

Place of birth **Brighton, UK**

Launched first company **Early 1980s**

Approximate wealth **£165 million**

Love him or loathe him, Simon Cowell is the judge every act wants to impress on his many TV talent shows. But it is his sharp business mind that has seen him rise to the very top of the music industry today.

POST ROOM BOY

Simon Cowell's music career started at EMI Music Publishing where he worked in the post room. Cowell worked his way up and left EMI in the early 1980s to become a **music publisher**. He worked with the owner of pop record label Fanfare, Iain Burton, and had hits with pop band Hot Gossip and singer Sinitta. Determined to succeed, he learned as much as he could about the music business from record producer Pete Waterman.

FRESH TALENT

Simon Cowell then began to scout for new talent. In the late 1990s he discovered, and signed, hugely successful boy band Westlife. Cowell first came to the public's attention in 2001 as a judge in a TV talent show called *Pop Idol*. He then showed his business sense by grabbing an opportunity – he took the best parts of the show and created and sold his own talent show, *The X Factor*, to ITV.

HITS AND MISSES

Cowell admits he has made mistakes during his career – for example, he turned down both the Spice Girls and Take That. But he says that he has learnt from his failures. His company Syco, a TV production and music publishing house, has been very successful. Cowell also developed the Got Talent reality TV format. *Britain's Got Talent* now has spin-off series all over the world. *The X Factor* continues to grow in popularity and has produced international stars, such as Leona Lewis. During the 2000s Cowell made a name for himself in the USA as a judge on the hit TV show *American Idol*. He has since launched *The X Factor* in the USA in 2011.

Simon Cowell has made three guest appearances in episodes of *The Simpsons*.

FACT

In 1989, due to business difficulties at Fanfare, Cowell became **bankrupt**. At the age of 30, he ended up moving back in with his parents.

SIR RICHARD BRANSON

CELEB BIO

Date of birth **18 July 1950**

Place of birth **London, UK**

Launched first company **1970**

Approximate wealth **£2.5 billion**

Wearing butterfly wings, billionaire businessman Sir Richard Branson runs in the London Marathon to raise money for charity.

The dynamic Sir Richard Branson is one of the world's greatest entrepreneurs. Always ready to take risks, he has grabbed many business opportunities to expand his Virgin empire into the global **brand** that it is today.

Richard Branson celebrates Virgin Atlantic's first flight to Mumbai International Airport in India.

HUGE HIT

In 1970 Branson founded Virgin as a **mail-order** record **retailer**. He then opened a record shop in London's Oxford Street. In 1973, a musician named Mike Oldfield was struggling to find a record label that would release his album *Tubular Bells*. Branson decided to set up his own record label and give Oldfield a chance. *Tubular Bells* was a massive Number One hit and put Virgin Records on the map. Virgin went on to sign major acts, including The Rolling Stones and The Sex Pistols. Branson sold the Virgin label to EMI for £500 million in 1992.

SUCCESS STORY

Branson went on to expand the Virgin Group into areas such as travel, leisure, tourism, **communications**, media, **finance** and health. In the late 1970s a flight that Branson was due to take was cancelled. He hired a plane for $2,000 (£1,200) and started selling tickets for $39 (£24) each to his fellow passengers. He filled every seat on the plane. This inspired him to launch his own airline, Virgin Atlantic Airlines, which he did in 1984.

GLOBAL BRAND

In 1999 Branson entered the mobile phone business. Virgin pay-as-you-go phones were an instant hit with young people in the UK. He launched Virgin Mobile USA in 2001 and it became the fastest company in history to generate **revenues** of over a billion dollars – in under three years. Virgin is now a global brand, with around 200 different companies in over 30 countries.

WATCH THIS SPACE

Richard Branson has written several books about his life's work and achievements. He continues to invest in new ideas and likes to follow his gut instinct. In 2004 Branson launched Virgin Galactic. With it he plans to pursue space tourism and create the world's first commercial spaceline!

FACT

Branson is the only person to have built eight billion-dollar companies from nothing in eight different business **sectors**.

'Business opportunities are like buses, there's always another one coming.'

Duncan Bannatyne has risen to the top of the business world despite his tough upbringing.

'I learned early that business and opportunity aren't handed to you on a plate and that you have to make your own chances.'

DUNCAN BANNATYNE

Duncan Bannatyne is a well-known face on TV as a formidable 'dragon' on the hit show *Dragons' Den*. Worth over £300 million, his business empire includes a chain of health clubs and hotels. He claims to be living proof that 'anyone can do it'.

DREAMS OF A BIKE

Bannatyne had a poor and tough childhood living near Glasgow, in Scotland. He decided to get a paper round so that he could buy himself a bike. His local newsagent said he had to find 100 new customers to create a round for himself. Young Bannatyne knocked on 150 doors to get his 100 addresses. And he bought his own bike.

IN THE NAVY

At 15 Bannatyne joined the Navy, **volunteering** for 12 years. By the time he was 18, he was very unhappy and wanted to leave. He decided the best way out, was to get into trouble, so he tried to throw his commanding officer overboard. Bannatyne served 18 months in a Military Corrective Training Centre before he received a **dishonourable discharge** from the Navy.

SELLING ICE CREAMS

In his twenties Bannatyne had a string of dead-end jobs. He found his first business opportunity at the age of 30. He bought an ice cream van at a car **auction** for £450. Duncan's Super Ices went from strength to strength and he later sold the business for £28,000. Bannatyne's next **venture** was to found a successful **nursing home** business. He soon became a multi-millionaire.

HEALTHY FUTURE

Bannatyne sold his nursing home business in 1997. He invested the money in setting up Bannatyne's Fitness Ltd, the UK's largest chain of independent health clubs. Today he has many business interests, including bars, hotels and property, as well as the Bannatyne Charitable Trust which gives money to a variety of good causes across the world. His job as a TV 'dragon' is to invest in strong business ideas put forward by Britain's budding entrepreneurs.

CELEB BIO

Date of birth **2 February 1949**

Place of birth **Clydebank, Scotland, UK**

Launched first company **1979**

Approximate wealth **£320 million**

FACT

Duncan Bannatyne received the Officer of the Order of the British Empire (**OBE** award) in 2004 for his contribution to charity.

Bannatyne (top left) takes part in the launch of a *Dragons' Den* book with his TV co-stars.

ROSS BRAWN

Ross Brawn has proved himself to be one of the top **engineers** in Formula 1 racing. A brilliant race **strategist** while at Honda, he famously decided to buy the company rather than see it shut down. This quiet man is clearly someone who means business.

ENGINEER

Brawn began his career in motor sport in 1976 at March Engineering, operating a machine that cut and shaped metal. Soon afterwards he became a mechanic for its Formula 3 racing team. He quickly worked his way up in the sport, joining the F1 Williams team in 1978. In the 1990s and 2000s Brawn was the technical director and **tactical** genius behind Formula 1 driver Michael Schumacher's seven world titles for car constructors Benetton and Ferrari.

HEAD OF HONDA

Brawn became team principal for Honda F1 in 2008. He was responsible for designing, manufacturing and engineering Honda's team car. However, in December that year, Honda announced its shock withdrawal from Formula 1 due to financial difficulties.

RELUCTANT ENTREPRENEUR

With a strong team and car, Brawn saw that this was a good business opportunity. But he could not find a buyer for the company. He decided to buy Honda F1 himself, renaming it Brawn GP. Brawn GP went on to win the 2009 F1 World **Constructors' Championship**, and British driver Jenson Button became the 2009 F1 World Champion. Brawn sold his F1 team to Mercedes in November 2009 in a deal worth around £110 million. Within a year, Brawn had made himself lots of money and secured the future of the team. Brawn continued as technical director of the Mercedes GP team.

Jenson Button leads the pack in the Monaco Grand Prix in Brawn GP's 2009 championship-winning season.

FACT

Brawn GP were the first team to win the F1 Championship on their debut.

'*... even with my long career in motor racing... I've genuinely never experienced anything like this.*'

[on Brawn GP's 2009 season]

Ross Brawn strolls down the pit lane at the Malaysian Grand Prix.

Mercedes-Benz

HENRI LLOYD

PETRONAS

BRIDGESTONE

CELEB BIO

Date of birth **23 November 1954**

Place of birth **Manchester, UK**

Launched first company **2009**

Approximate wealth **£100–150 million**

JAMIE OLIVER

Jamie Oliver is one of the UK's best-loved TV chefs, renowned for his relaxed presenting style. He is also a successful restaurant owner and clever businessman. Incredibly passionate about food, he campaigns for people to cook more healthily with fresh ingredients.

CHEEKY CHEF

Oliver's parents, who run a country pub, inspired Jamie at an early age with their love of food. Oliver left school at 16 and began training as a chef. He worked as a sous-chef at River Café in London, in charge of cooking food in a busy kitchen. In 1999 he was spotted as a future talent by a TV producer and landed his own series for the BBC. Oliver's confident, cheeky personality meant that his series *The Naked Chef* was a big hit. He then signed a lucrative deal with supermarket Sainsbury's to front their advertising campaign. By the age of 24, Oliver was a millionaire.

CHARITY WORK

Oliver often combines his entrepreneurial skill with his will to improve people's lives in some way. In 2002 Oliver wanted to help disadvantaged teenagers. He launched a restaurant called Fifteen where he showed 15 youngsters from difficult backgrounds how to become chefs. The TV series *Jamie's Kitchen* charted the ups and downs of this tricky business venture. The first restaurant proved a success, and other Fifteen restaurants have now opened around the world.

FOOD CAMPAIGNER

Jamie Oliver is a passionate man. In the TV show *Jamie's School Dinners*, he campaigned to improve school menus around the UK. He swapped sausages and chips for tasty, healthy pastas and salads. He showed people the changes they needed to make to their diet through his cookery programmes and further campaign shows such as *Jamie's Food Revolution USA*. The Jamie Oliver brand just keeps growing.

The celebrity chef adds finishing touches to promote his *Jamie's Dinners* TV show in Germany.

Jamie Oliver dresses up as peas in a pod in a school canteen to put forward his message of healthy eating.

Jamie Oliver's many TV series have been great success stories. The accompanying cookbooks are best-sellers all over the world and have been translated into 29 different languages.

DAS
JAMIE
OLIVER
DINNER

'I have a fairly low regard for money to be honest. However, if… you haven't got money and you've got a great idea, it's hard to get it done.'

CELEB BIO

Date of birth	**27 May 1975**
Place of birth	**Southend, Essex, UK**
Launched first company	**2002**
Approximate wealth	**£65 million**

KATIE PRICE

Once a glamour model known as Jordan, Katie Price is constantly in the headlines and gossip columns of tabloid newspapers and magazines. But behind the image, Katie Price is a smart businesswoman – and one of Britain's richest female celebrities.

JORDAN

Price burst onto the celebrity scene as a young glamour model and dated a string of celebrities, including high-profile footballers. Her appearance on reality TV show *I'm A Celebrity... Get Me Out of Here!* in 2004 also helped to raise her profile. Over the years Price has continued to expose her private life in the media, but she has been shrewd and used this to her advantage.

PROMOTING HERSELF

Price has created a unique brand by exploiting her celebrity. Critics often state that she is simply 'famous for being famous', having no particular talent. However, the selling power of the Katie Price brand cannot be denied. With the help of a **ghostwriter**, Price has written several best-selling autobiographies and has released successful children's and adult fiction. Her 2009 novel *Sapphire* topped the hardback book charts for four weeks running. She has also launched a wide variety of top-selling products, including clothing, jewellery, perfumes and lingerie.

I'M A CELEBRITY...

Price's true entrepreneurial skill appears to be self-promotion. By keeping herself in the limelight she can promote her new business ventures. A recent survey also suggests that, as a celebrity entrepreneur, Katie Price is more likely to inspire young women than more traditional female role models.

'If you don't try then you'll never succeed... Just go for it – that's always my motto.'

Katie Price models at the launch of her new perfume.

FACT

Katie Price understands the power and value of her celebrity status better than most. She is reputed to have demanded £1.75 million from *OK!* magazine for exclusive pictures of her wedding to singer Peter Andre in 2005.

Katie Price attends a book
signing for her autobiography
You Only Live Once.

CELEB BIO

Date of birth	**22 May 1978**
Place of birth	**Brighton, UK**
Launched first company	**2005**
Approximate wealth	**£40 million**

MARK ZUCKERBERG

CELEB BIO

Date of birth	**14 May 1984**
Place of birth	**Dobbs Ferry, New York, USA**
Launched first company	**2004**
Approximate wealth	**£4.3 billion**

Mark Zuckerberg announces a new email messaging system for Facebook. Zuckerberg is constantly trying to improve and grow the company.

> *'One of the things I think about every day is how do we make this company move as quickly as possible. That's a really big deal.'*

Actor Jesse Eisenberg (left) played Zuckerberg in the award-winning film *The Social Network* (see below).

Mark Zuckerberg is the real face behind the global social network phenomenon known as Facebook. The company is just one of the many projects of the skilled young software developer who has become one of the greatest Internet entrepreneurs.

COLLEGE COMMUNICATION

Mark Zuckerberg created Facebook in February 2004 while still at university at Harvard in the USA. The social networking site grew out of his own computer project, which was co-founded by his Harvard University room-mates Dustin Moskovitz and Chris Hughes, and friend Eduardo Saverin. The idea was a simple form of communication – putting students in touch with each other to share things they had in common.

OPENING IT UP

Initially, Facebook was just for Harvard students, but Zuckerberg gradually made it open to other US universities. The word soon spread. Zuckerberg left university with co-founder Moskovitz

and moved to California to concentrate on developing Facebook. In 2005 Facebook began to add international networks. The company continued to grow rapidly. By 2008 it had 100 million active users. By January 2011 this number had swelled to 600 million.

BEHIND THE FACE

The 2010 film *The Social Network* claims to be the story of Facebook's founding years. Mark Zuckerberg has described the film as inaccurate. However, at the 2011 Golden Globe Awards it won five **gongs**, including Best Motion Picture.

CONNECTING THE WORLD

Some major businesses have attempted to buy Facebook because of the explosive

growth in the number of users. Zuckerberg has always refused to sell the company. To him Facebook is more about fun than business. He explains that his mission is to make the world more open, allowing information to flow from person to person. He remains **chief executive officer (CEO)** and president of Facebook.

FACT

Within one year Facebook doubled its number of users – it jumped from 250 million active users in July 2009 to 500 million users in July 2010.

VICTORIA BECKHAM

As a pouting young pop star she championed 'Girl Power'. Now married with children, Victoria Beckham has matured into an enduring style icon. Half of one of the most famous couples in the world, she is known for her own business achievements in fashion.

Victoria Beckham models one of the dresses from her own Autumn 2010 collection.

POP STAR

In the late 1990s, Victoria Adams forged a remarkable career as 'Posh Spice' in girl band The Spice Girls. Although her own solo pop music career was not considered a glittering success, she released four UK Top 10 singles between 2001 and 2003.

STYLE ICON

Posh married Manchester United footballer David Beckham in 1999. As his career rocketed into superstardom, the attractive couple became known worldwide as style icons. Having settled into motherhood, Victoria began to seek out a new career path and turned her attention to fashion.

CELEBRITY ENTREPRENEUR

Victoria Beckham has always seized the opportunities of fame. Recognized and photographed by the world's **paparazzi**, she knows how to dress stylishly and turn heads. In 2004 she designed a limited-edition line of jeans for Rock & Republic. This unleashed her entrepreneurial side, and she created her own denim brand, dVb Style. She also released a best-selling style guide called *That Extra Half an Inch: hair, heels and everything in between*.

FASHION DESIGNER

Victoria Beckham's business venture has grown in recent years to include her own range of dresses, sunglasses, handbags and jewellery. She has also launched a collection of successful 'his and her' fragrances with her husband, David. A celebrity for over a decade, Victoria Beckham is now making her mark as a fashion designer and serious entrepreneur.

'I am a perfectionist and a control freak. I giv 110 per cent when I go to work, and I expect that from the people that work with me.'

Even a trip to the shops is a chance to dress glamorously for Victoria Beckham – and her son Cruz!

FACT

In 2007, Beckham won two British *Glamour* Magazine Awards, one for 'Woman of the Year' and the other for 'Entrepreneur of the Year', which celebrated her fashion achievements.

CELEB BIO

Date of birth **17 April 1974**

Place of birth **Goffs Oak, Hertfordshire, UK**

Launched first company **2006**

Approximate wealth **£145 million (joint fortune with husband David)**

BILL GATES

Bill Gates speaks at a Health Summit in Washington DC, USA.

'It's fine to celebrate success but it is more important to heed the lessons of failure.'

Bill Gates is given a warm welcome in India after announcing he is to give 100 million dollars to help people in the country suffering from the illness HIV/AIDS.

Bill Gates is a self-made billionaire – many, many times over. He manufactured the Windows operating system that is seen on computers all over the world. He is now a household name and one of the most generous people in the world, giving much of his wealth away to charity.

EARLY DAYS

A bright pupil who was good at maths and science, Bill Gates quickly became a computer-mad teenager in the early 1970s. Teaching himself from a handbook, he learnt to write **computer code**. By the age of 17, he had already sold his first computer program.

MICROSOFT IS BORN

Gates worked with fellow student Paul Allen at Harvard University to write the first computer program for a **PC**. Gates gave up university in 1975 at the age of 19 to found Microsoft. His vision for the future was to put a computer on every office desk and in every home.

BIG BUSINESS

In 1980 the computer giant IBM asked Microsoft to write a computer program for a new PC. Gates also provided IBM with an operating system, called MS-DOS. In partnership with IBM, Gates then developed an improved operating system in 1984 called Microsoft Windows.

By 1986, aged only 31, Bill Gates was the youngest person to become a billionaire. Microsoft has continued to release profitable products. In 2001 it launched the Xbox video game console. From 1995 to 2007 Gates was officially the wealthiest man in the world.

TRUST WORK

Bill Gates has chosen to use his enormous wealth to help others who are less fortunate. In 1999, he set up a **charitable** trust called the Bill and Melinda Gates Foundation. Its aim is to support education and health projects across the world. Today the Foundation is one of the world's largest charitable trusts.

FACT

About 90 per cent of the world's computers currently run on Bill Gates' Microsoft Windows operating system.

CELEB BIO

Date of birth **28 October 1955**

Place of birth **Seattle, Washington, USA**

Launched first company **1975**

Approximate wealth **£33 billion**

GLOSSARY

auction A public sale in which goods are sold to the highest bidder.

bankrupt A person is bankrupt when the courts decide that they cannot afford to pay their debts.

brand Name or symbol that marks a business as different from similar products or services provided by other businesses.

campaign To carry out work to achieve a certain goal.

charitable Relating to the giving of money or help to those who need it.

chief executive officer (CEO) The highest-ranking executive, or person with authority, in a company.

civil service Jobs in government administration.

communications A system of sending messages such as telephone, mail or Internet.

computer code Arrangement of data or instructions in a computer program.

Constructors' Championship Award to the most successful Formula 1 constructor, or race car team, based on the team's results during a Grand Prix season.

dishonourable discharge Dismissal from the military for really bad behaviour.

engineer A person skilled in designing, building or maintaining engines, cars or machines.

entrepreneur Someone who takes the risk in a business enterprise or venture.

finance The management of large amounts of money.

ghostwriter A person whose job it is to write material for someone else who is the named author.

gong An award.

icon A person regarded with admiration.

investment Money put into a business.

lucrative Producing a healthy profit.

mail-order A business that delivers orders by post.

media Different types of communications, including the Internet, newspapers, TV and radio.

mogul A rich or powerful business person.

music publisher Someone who markets and promotes the songs or music of songwriters. Music publishers also make sure songwriters are paid when their music is played in public.

nursing home A building used for the care of elderly or very ill people.

OBE An award presented by the Queen to individuals in the UK recognising their outstanding achievement or services.

paparazzi Italian word used for photographers who chase after celebrities to take shots they can sell to magazines and newspapers.

PC Short for 'personal computer'.

phenomenon Something marvellous or astonishing.

receiver box A device connecting a TV with an outside signal, for example for satellite TV.

retailer Someone who sells goods directly to the customer.

revenues Sources of income, or money coming in.

ruthless Without pity or mercy.

sector An area of business that is different from others.

shrewd Smart, or with a sharp intelligence.

social network A website that allows users to communicate directly with each other.

software Programs used by a computer.

spin-off A different version that is based on a popular show.

strategist Expert in strategy, or planning.

tabloid A small, colourful newspaper with entertaining and exciting stories.

tactical Using tactics or special skills.

venture A project where you hope to make a profit.

volunteering Offering to do something without being asked.

FURTHER INFORMATION

BOOKS

Graphic Biographies: Oprah Winfrey by Gary Jeffrey (Franklin Watts, 2009)

Inspirational Lives: Jamie Oliver by Liz Gogerly (Wayland, 2010)

Inspirational Lives: Richard Branson by Liz Gogerly (Wayland, 2010)

Inspirational Lives: Simon Cowell by Debbie Foy (Wayland, 2010)

Inspirational Lives: The Beckhams by Liz Gogerly (Wayland, 2010)

DVDS [& BLU-RAY]

Dragons' Den Complete BBC Series 1 & 2 (Odeon Entertainment, 2008)

Formula One Season Review 2009 [with extra features including Back from the Brink with BRAWN GP] (2 Entertain, 2009)

The Social Network (Sony Pictures Home Entertainment, 2010)

WEBSITES

www.bbc.co.uk/apprentice/

Official website of the popular TV series *The Apprentice* starring Lord Sugar.

www.bbc.co.uk/dragonsden/

Official website of *Dragons' Den*. Meet the business dragons, including Duncan Bannatyne, as well as the show's budding entrepreneurs.

www.facebook.com/press/info.php?timeline

Check out the timeline of Facebook – the world's biggest social networking site.

www.jamieoliver.com

Find out more about the Jamie Oliver Foundation, the *Food Revolution* and *School Dinners*.

www.virgin.com

Discover more about Sir Richard Branson and the Virgin brand.

INDEX

FALKIRK COUNCIL
LIBRARY SUPPORT
FOR SCHOOLS